MW01286082

FOR A POSITIVE CRITIQUE

FOR A POSITIVE CRITIQUE

BY A MILITANT / FOR OTHER MILITANTS

Written by Dominique Venner

ARKTOS
LONDON 2017

Copyright © 2017 by Arktos Media Ltd.

All rights reserved. No part of this book may be reproduced or utilised in any form or by any means (whether electronic or mechanical), including photocopying, recording or by any information storage and retrieval system, without permission in writing from the publisher.

Printed in the United Kingdom.

ISBN	978-1-912079-84-1 (Paperback)
	978-1-912079-83-4 (Ebook)
TRANSLATION & EDITING	Aodren Guillermou
COVER AND LAYOUT	Tor Westman
ORIGINAL TITLE	*Pour une critique positive* (c. 1964)

www.arktos.com

// CONTENTS

The Flaws of the "Nationalist" Opposition   1

Conceptual Defects   2
Ideological Confusion   2
Conformism   2
Archaism   3

Organizational Defects   3
Opportunism   3
Mythomania   4
Terrorism   5
Anarchism   5

For a New Revolutionary Theory   9

There are no Spontaneous Revolutions   10
A Revolutionary Consciousness   13
No Revolutionary Doctrine, no Revolution!   15

Nationalist Perspectives   19

Critique of Liberalism and Marxism   19
A Virile Humanism   22
A Living Order   23
An Organic Economy   25
A Young Europe   27

Organization and Action

Notables or Militants 35

For a Man or an Idea? 35

Bluffing and Effectiveness 36

The Notables and the Rank and File 36

Union of "Nationals" or Organization of Revolutionaries 37

Hidden Enemies 37

Zero plus Zero 39

Unions and Committees of Agreement 39

Monolithic and Disciplined Organization 40

Plots or Popular Action 41

Behind the Times 41

A Thousand Revolutionary Cadres 42

On the Occidental Scale 44

An Exterior Lung 44

Solidarity and Orchestration 44

New Blood 45

To Begin 46

Theatrical Revolutionaries 47

Bases Among People 48

Craft Industry or Effectiveness 49

Craft Industry 49

Division of Labor and Centralization 50

THE FLAWS OF THE "NATIONALIST" OPPOSITION

The action undertaken after the failure of April 1961 has made use of new means. It has mobilized a greater number of partisans and has resolutely pursued a violent and clandestine path. This transformation of the forms of struggle, however, has not affected the fundamentals of the methods that preceded it. It continues to conform to the characteristics of "nationalist" struggles, fraught with both courage and failure.

In 1917, Lenin ran the risk of military defeat in order to create the conditions of the Bolshevik revolution. Franco marked his grip over the insurrectional command in 1936 by executing his own cousin, who refused to follow him. These are two examples of behavior opposite to that of the "nationalists."

By contrast, the refusal to actually bring the fight to Metropolitan France on April 22, 1961, such as during the bloody and futile Parisian demonstration of February 6, 1934, is typical of the "nationalist" mentality.

Conceptual Defects

These "nationalists" who use the word "revolution," without knowing its meaning, believe there will be some spontaneous "nationalist awakening." They also believe in the army's support. They trust in these unrealizable dreams as one trusts dubious miracle cures, they do not understand the necessity of educating partisans with sound doctrine that explains the causes of Western decadence, proposes a solution, and serves as a guidepost for thought and action. Thus they wallow in a string of political afflictions that are ultimately responsible for their failures.

Ideological Confusion

The "nationalists" attack the symptoms of the disease, not the cause. They are anti-communists, but forget that neo-liberal capitalist regimes are the primary vectors of communism. They are hostile to the government's Algerian policy, but forget that this policy was the product of a particular regime, its ideology, interests, real financial masters and technocrats, as well as its political and economic structures. They sought to save French Algeria from this regime, while still buying into its myths and tenets. Can you imagine the early Christians worshiping pagan idols and communists praising capitalism?

Conformism

Every "nationalist" has his good Gaullist, his good technocrat, his good minister. Yielding to old bourgeois reflexes, he dreads "the adventure" and "the chaos." As long as men of the regime wave the flag, he will trust them. He prefers the comfort of self-deception to lucidity. Sentimentalism and parochial interests always prevail over political reasoning. In the vain hope of satisfying everybody, refuses to take a side and ultimately satisfies nobody.

Archaism

For lack of imagination, the "nationalists" continue to blow Déroulède's bugle, which rallies but a scant few. Programs and slogans are fixed to the pre-war tricolor. Everything from military takeovers to negative anti-communism, through to counter-revolution and corporatism, these "nationalist formulas" repel more than they attract. This political arsenal is half a century old. It has no hold on our people.

Organizational Defects

The same reasons for which these "nationalists" reject the primary importance of ideas in the context of a political struggle result in their complete rejection of organization. Their actions are vitiated by the very flaws that are their undoing.

Opportunism

Many noteworthy nationalists, including members of parliament and those in the military and civilian sectors, are opportunists as a matter of personal ambition. They generally camouflage their careerism in the skills that they bring to the table. It is using these skills that the "nationalists" supported the referendum of 1958 and the enterprises of politicians ever since. Behind each of these positions, they see the prospect of a medal, a sinecure, or an election. They can feel the changes in the wind and may become violent, even seditious, when doing so appears to be profitable. Their violent speeches frighten no one. They may attack a man, or the government, but they are careful not to attack the core of the regime itself. Algeria served as a springboard, a chance to make a fortune from the generously dispensed subsidies, while the militants had to fight with their bare hands. If the wind turns, they do not hesitate to betray their flag and their comrades. Their seat in parliament is not a means but an end in itself: it must be kept at all costs. The lowly partisan is opportunistic by lack of doctrine and training. He trusts the smooth talker and his superficial impressions rather than analysis of political ideas and facts, he is dedicated to being duped.

Mythomania

The reading of far too many spy novels, memories of the Resistance and other special services, not to mention plotters, Gaullists and others, plunge the "nationalists" into a state of permanent reverie. A game of bridge with a retired general, a member of parliament, or a sergeant from the army reserve becomes a dark and powerful conspiracy. If they recruit as few as ten high school students, they think themselves Mussolini. If they boast that they command a group of five thousand organized men, it means they merely have a ragtag mob of several hundred. If, by chance, they receive a letter from a military institution, they display the envelope with ominous sighs and silences, as if involved in some cloak and dagger conspiracy. They call for unity but have only bitter reproaches against the sectarianism of militants who refuse to take them seriously. These same "nationalists," in periods of genuine repression, are arrested with lists of addresses and documents, and begin to talk the moment the policeman raises his voice.

Terrorism

Inept situational analysis, and the absence of doctrine and training that pushes some towards opportunism, throws others into counterproductive violence and terrorism. Poor understanding of the most basic studies, as well as devotion to certain aspects of the communist subversion of the FLN has increased this tendency. The detonators set under the concierges' windows did not bring a single partisan to the cause of French Algeria. Blind terrorism is the best way to alienate the general population. As indispensable as clandestine action and the calculated use of force can be when a nation has no other means of defending itself, especially when this action seeks to call the populace to action, terrorism places those using it outside the popular community and is condemned to failure.

Anarchism

The "nationalists" who admire the discipline of others are, in practice, essentially anarchists. Unable to identify their place in the struggle, they have a taste for disorderly action. Their vanity pushes them to gratuitous individual acts, even if their cause suffers from it. They ignore their word of honor and nobody can predict where their fantasies will lead them. They rigorously follow a ringleader and thrive in small clans. The absence of common ideological references increases their scattering and their organizational unity.

FOR A NEW REVOLUTIONARY THEORY

Before we attempt to define a constructive solution, a critique of "nationalist" flaws is indispensable. Some, for lack of political maturity, will not be able to comprehend it. Those who have drawn upon the lessons of their own experience, however, will understand this necessity.

Revolution is not just the violence that is sometimes involved in a political takeover. Nor is it a simple change of institutions or political cliques. Revolution is not the seizure of power, it is the use of power to construct a new society.

Such a task is unimaginable in the face of disordered thought and action. It requires immense preparation and training. The "nationalist" struggle is stuck in the same ruts it was a half-century ago. Before anything else can be done, a new revolutionary theory must be developed.

There are no Spontaneous Revolutions

It is always easy to act, it is less easy to succeed. This is especially true of revolutionary struggles, in a fight to the death against an all-powerful, cunning, and experienced enemy, which must be fought with ideas and with cunning before it can be fought with force. It is common for some, however, to pit thought against action. To do so is to believe in the spontaneity of revolutionary action. The example of the Fascist revolution in Italy is cited. One forgets that when the "fascios" were formed in 1919, Mussolini had been fighting for more than twelve years as an agitator and journalist. One also forgets that the conditions of the struggle in Italy after the armistice of 1918, are nothing like the conditions in France today.

In Italy, like many other European Nations, the power of the State was extremely weak and totally incapable of imposing its law on the armed factions which were fighting over the country. The State had to deal with each of these veritable political armies as they cropped up. In October 1922, the blackshirts were the strongest and thus managed to assume control of the state. Today, the "liberal regimes" of the West are characterized by a large privileged caste, which serves as an agent of financial groups, who control all the political, administrative, and economic levers, united in their complicity. They can rely on gigantic administrative devices that rigorously oversees the population, especially through the social services sector. They hold a monopoly over political and economic power. They control most of the media and are the masters of thought. They are protected by vast police forces. They have turned their people into obedient little sheep. Only controlled opposition is tolerated.

At the end of the First World War, communist revolution was an immediate threat to all of Europe. The nature of a threat determines how one responds: fascist movements saw a chance and took it. Being the only force capable of opposing Red violence, fascism received powerful support and the adherence of a large number of partisans. Today, the factory Soviets, the Chekas, belong to the past. The communists of the West have become gentrified, they are simply a part of the scenery and they are the firmest defenders of the regime. "The man with a knife between his teeth" is no longer the communist but the activist. As for Russia, capitalists see nothing but new markets there.

Unlike the first half of the twentieth century, basic material needs are within the reach of all. The soup kitchens and the wildcat strikes are forgotten. Save a few threatened minorities, the vast majority of wage-earners are convinced that they have more to lose than to gain by violently taking what peaceful demands and time will inevitably give them. The yoke of social laws and blackmail by credit keep the rest from causing a ruckus.

These days, the greater good, as well as civic and political courage are limited to a small minority, whose legal means of expression have been systematically reduced. This is leagues away from Italy in the 1920s. The personal genius of Mussolini was sufficient to gather and mobilize a passionate mass and to conquer a State incapable of defending itself. The situation in Europe and in France is no longer conducive to this type of action. Since power belongs to the adversary, a superior cunning is required. Since the "great man" (besides being nonexistent) has greatly depreciated, one must rely on his team. That is, the quality of comrades and methodical, well-reasoned struggle. In this, education and doctrine are essential.

Since 1947, France has fought to defend its overseas territories, was victorious in the field, but was forced into successive capitulations by the political and economic forces that constitute the regime. It was not until the month of April 1961, fourteen years, that a few small cadres of men were able to discern their true enemies. An enemy who was not so much in the field, under the guise of a Viet or of a *fellagha*[1], but rather in France itself, in the boards of directors, the banks, the editorial offices, the assemblies, and the ministerial offices. Once again, this hostility was directed against the mythical decadent Metropolitan France rather than the reality of the regime.

To conquer, it is important to understand the reality of the regime, to learn its methods, to flush out its accomplices, especially those camouflaged as patriots. We must find positive solutions that will allow for the construction of a new society. This necessitates a thorough self-scrutiny, a thorough review of accepted truths, in short, a revolutionary consciousness.

---

1   Arabic for "bandit." Referring to groups of armed militants affiliated with anti-colonial movements in French North Africa.

A Revolutionary Consciousness

There is nothing less spontaneous than a revolutionary consciousness. The revolutionary is wholly conscious of the struggle between Nationalism, bearer of the creative and spiritual values of the West, and Materialism under its liberal or Marxist forms. He is free of the prejudices, falsehoods, and the conditioned reflexes with which the regime defends itself. The political education with which one frees himself of these is obtained through personal experience, of course, but especially through the kind learning that one can only acquire through study. Without such an education, even the most courageous and most audacious man becomes a puppet manipulated by the regime. As circumstances dictate, the regime pulls the strings that regulate his behavior: patriotism, blind anti-communism, the fascist menace, legalism, the unity of the army, etc. Using the permanent one-way propaganda, to which everybody is subjected from childhood, the regime, in all its forms, has progressively intoxicated the French people. This is true of all democratic nations at this point. Any critical thought, any personal opinion is destroyed. The moment those keywords that trigger their conditioned reflex are uttered, all reason is thrown out the window.

Spontaneity feeds this conditioned reflex. It leads only to revolts, which are very easy to defuse or to divert with only a few superficial concessions, a few bones to chew on, or a few changes of scenery. And so it was time and time again with the French Algerians, the army, and the "nationalists."

In the face of mortal danger, it is possible to set up a defensive front. Both the Resistance at the end of the last war and the OAS are perfect examples. The outcome of the fight was a question of life or death; the physical struggle against a very tangible adversary is often a pitiless one. Supposing that a revolt were to triumph, as soon as the enemy is vanquished, the once united front explodes into multiple clans, and the mass of partisans, having no more reason to fight, returns to its everyday life, demobilizes, and entrusts the city they have liberated to those who lost it in the first place.

France and Europe must accomplish their nationalist revolution in order to survive. Superficial changes will not strike at the heart of the evil. Nothing will change until the weeds of this regime are extirpated down to the last root. To achieve this, we must destroy its political organization, overthrow its idols and dogmas, eliminate both its official and secret masters, and show the people the extent to which they have been deceived and exploited. Then, reconstruction can begin. Not based on paper tigers, but on a young and revolutionary elite, imbued with a new conception of the world. Is such revolutionary action conceivable without the direction of a sound revolutionary doctrine? Certainly not. How can you oppose an adversary armed with a well-tested dialectic, rich with long experience, that is powerfully organized, and without ideology or method?

No Revolutionary Doctrine, no Revolution!

Even at the military stage, the revolutionary struggle is above all psychological. How is it to be conducted, how are partisans to be converted and inspired without a clear definition of the new ideology, without doctrine? A doctrine understood, not as ideological abstractions, but as a rudder for thought and action.

Maintaining the moral offensive among its own partisans and communicating its convictions to waverers, are two indispensable conditions for the development of Nationalism. It has been proven that in action or in prison, when demoralization is close at hand and the adversary seems to have won, the educated militants, whose faith is fueled by coherent thinking, have superior powers of resistance.

The development of new doctrine is the only answer to the divisions between activists. There is no doubt about the unifying value of action. But this unification lasting nor practical without ideological unification around a sound doctrine. The editor of *France-Observateur*, SFIO officials, and communists, all share the same ideology: Marxism. Their ideological reference is therefore the same, their worldview is similar. The words they use have the same meaning. They belong to the same family. Despite the profound differences in their methods, they all apply the same ideology. This is not true of their nationalist opposition. Our activists do not share any common ancestors. Some are fascistic, others are Maurrasians, others still are Integrists, and all these categories contain many variants. Their only point of unity is what they are against: communism, Gaullism, etc. They do not understand each other. The words that they use — revolution, counter-revolution, nationalism, Europe, etc. — have different, indeed opposite meanings. How can they not oppose each other? How can they stand united with such differences in worldview? Revolutionary unity is impossible without unity of doctrine.

The works of Marx are immense, unreadable, and obscure. A Lenin was needed to extract a clear doctrine and to transform this enormous hotchpotch into an effective weapon of political war. Nationalism has its own collective Marx, just as obscure and unsuitable as Engels' partner was for Russia in 1903. It is imperative that we create our own Lenin.

Nationalism is the heir to an infinitely rich body of thought, but it is too diverse, incomplete, and tainted by archaism. The time has come to synthesize this body of work, and to supplement it with qualifying statements required to explain new problems. For example, a documented analysis of High Finance, or of the Doctrines of Nationalism, are excellent examples of syntheses that respond to this need.

The causes that precipitated, the birth of Nationalism as a political ideology (and not simply the awakening of the national consciousness in a narrow sense) at the end of the nineteenth century, have not varied much from that time. Nationalism was born from the critique of liberal society in the nineteenth century. Later on, it fought against Marxism, the illegitimate child of liberalism.

Nationalism, coming after the counter-Encyclopédistes, after the Positivists, after Taine and Renan, whose teachings remain a part of Nationalist doctrine, Drumont and Barrès outlined the permanent characteristics of this ideology, to which Charles Maurras, José Antonio Primo de Rivera, Robert Brasillach, Alexis Carrel, and many others in Europe contributed their own ideas and genius. Founded on a heroic conception of life, Nationalism, which is a return to the source of popular community, intends to create new social relationships based on community and to build a political order based on the hierarchy of merit and value. Stripped from the narrow envelope imposed by a particular era, Nationalism has become a new political philosophy. European in its conceptions and its perspectives, it brings a universal solution to the problems facing mankind as a result of the technical revolution.

NATIONALIST PERSPECTIVES

The indifference of public opinion and the cowardice of traditional elites in the face of the Algerian question have opened the eyes of all men capable of reflection. Often at the price of painful revisions of their past convictions, they rally around a new definition of Nationalism. This is not the place to attempt a test of doctrine. Analyses and confrontations will be necessary. It is, however, possible to outline key propositions.

Critique of Liberalism and Marxism

Liberalism certainly had its charms, or appeared to, with its veneer of generosity. A veneer smashed by the hard truths of reality. This broken ideology serves as camouflage for the hypocritical dictatorship of international capitalism that rules over Western democracies.

The capitalist oligarchy was born at the end of the eighteenth century. In those days, liberalism was used in France to justify the combined interests of the high aristocracy and the rich against the central authority of that had kept them in check for so long. This struggle between large and popular power (in this case the French monarchy) re-occurs quite a bit throughout history. In organized societies, once the institutional veil of monarchism and of republicanism that hides reality has been stripped, two types of power can be discerned: the first one is based on the people through which large interests, be they feudal or financial, are contained, the second is in the hands of large interests so as to exploit the people. The first one identifies with the popular community and serves the destiny of the people, the second subjugates the popular community for the sole satisfaction of its appetite.

Modern democracies, which belong to the second type, have evolved alongside capitalism, in fact, they are but the latter's political emanation. Capitalism having shed its personal and financial skin, has become financial and stateless. Democratic nations have thus come under the control of international financial groups. The few differences that remain between the latter disappear as soon as the threat of a popular awakening appears. If the lies and the ruses they have mastered prove insufficient, they employ deadlier weapons, and more violent restraints. They have never recoiled in the face of genocide, atomic bombings, concentration camps, torture, or psychological rape.

The capitalist oligarchy is indifferent to the fate of national communities. Its goal is to satisfy an insatiable will to power through the economic domination of the world. Mankind and its civilizations are sacrificed upon the altar of its materialistic designs, which parallel those of Marxism. For technocrats and communists, man is but an economic animal endowed with two functions: produce and consume. What cannot be measured or calculated is considered superfluous. The superfluous must submit to what is deemed essential: economic output. Individualist tendencies, which do nothing but inconvenience the practical application of plans, must disappear. In materialist societies, there is only room for docile, homogeneous, and standardized masses.

Those who do not accept this brainwashing and who reject the castration of the masses are labeled "fascists." To doubt the sincerity of those who dictate opinion in a democracy or to challenge the contradictions of the "party line" in a communist regime, refusing to compare the culture of the West to the pre-historic wailing of negritude or the morbid decomposition of a certain modernism, despising the "universal conscience," smiling when one talks of the right of peoples to self-determination, are masters of a toxic and rebellious spirit. Rebellion leads to physical elimination in a communist regime and to social elimination in a liberal regime. Thus, the one and the other destroy creative individualism and popular roots, the very essence of mankind and its community. They bring humanity to a dead end, the worst kind of regression.

The history of mankind is one long struggle to liberate itself from the laws of matter. Religion, art, science, and ethics are all conquests of the spirit and of the human will. Man's victory in these fields has birthed entire civilizations. Arbitrary creations of the sensibilities, of the intelligence, and of the energy of peoples and civilizations develop and mature for as long as they maintain their creative power. The peoples who gave them birth lose the strength to defend themselves against external assaults when their original virtues and their vital energy disappear, and their civilization falls in turn into annihilation or decadence.

Such is the logical result of the exploitation of mankind by the caste of technocrats or by the "new ruling class." These two forces come from the same philosophy.

Liberalism and Marxism have taken different paths which have brought them to oppose each other but which lead to the same result: the subjection of people misled by the democratic myths. Democracy is the new opiate of the masses.

A Virile Humanism

The European people have built a unique civilization. Its creative power has not diminished. Even its enemies implicitly recognize its universality. Between the traditional East, which is submissive to metaphysical rules, and the new materialist societies, European civilization synthesizes spiritual aspirations and material necessities. Even when uniformity of the masses is proclaimed as an ideal everywhere in the world, it exalts the individualism of the strong, the triumph of human quality over mediocrity.

It represents the equilibrium to solve the upheavals created by the technical revolution. Founded on the values of the individual and the community, this harmony creates a kind of virile humanism.

As a new law tablet, this virile humanism rejects the false laws of numbers and seeks to submit the power of technique and of the economy to the civilizing will of the European man. This European man will rediscover within his lineage and in his true culture a world to his measure. He will discover the meaning of his life in the fulfillment of his own destiny, in his fidelity to a way of life founded on the European ethos of honor.

The ethos of honor opposes the slave morality of liberal or Marxist materialism. It affirms that life is a battle. It exalts the value of sacrifice. It believes in the power of the will. It bases the relationship between men of the same community on loyalty and solidarity. It gives work an importance independent of profit. It recovers a true sense of dignity to mankind, not given, but conquered through endless struggle. It gives European man an awareness of his responsibilities in relation to humanity, of which he is the natural organizer.

A Living Order

The legitimacy of power is not the result of eminently variable written laws nor of the consent of the masses obtained by means of propaganda. Power becomes legitimate when it respects the rights of the Nation, and the unwritten laws revealed by history.

Power is illegitimate when it deviates from a nation's destiny and destroys national realities. In such a situation, legitimacy belongs to those who struggle to restore the rights of their Nation.

As a lucid minority, they form the revolutionary elite upon which the future rests.

The world does not yield to a system, but to a will. Do not seek a system, seek the will. Of course, the very structure of the State must be based around some guiding principles: authority, continuity, and the power of design are combined in a collective form; one that must draw on a hierarchical corps of political cadres, assisted by a true popular representation of the professional and regional communities who are qualified to deliberate their own problems. But it is especially important to forge the men upon whom the community and the future of civilization will rest.

It is neither electronic equipment nor scholars that will decide the fate of humanity. The immense problems presented by new technical developments require a vocational political elite, endowed with an iron will that serves a historical mission. This overwhelming responsibility will, justifiably, demand more from them than from other men.

Sociologists claim that five percent of all people are profoundly perverted, crazy, or vicious. At the other extreme, one can observe the same proportion of men who possess, naturally well-developed qualities of spirit and self-sacrifice that predispose them to serve and lead the community. The democracies that prop up the reign of fraud and money are, in large part, dominated by the former. The Nationalist revolution will have to eliminate the former and impose the latter.

The selection and the education, from youth, of this elite, will be one of the primary preoccupations of the new society.

Their training will invigorate their character, develop their spirit of sacrifice, and will open their minds to intellectual disciplines. They will maintain their purity, not only by their commitment to honor, but to strict principles. They will form a living order, one constantly renewed over time, but always similar in spirit. Thus, the power of financiers will be replaced by that of believers and of warriors.

An Organic Economy

The economy is not an end in itself. It is but an element in the life of societies. It is neither the source nor the explanation of mankind's evolution. It is an agent, a consequence. It is in the psychology of peoples, in their energy, and in their political virtues that one finds the latter.

The economy must be subjected to political will. Should the latter disappear — as in liberal regimes — unchecked economic forces will drag society towards anarchy.

The immense economic question is naturally part of the Nationalist revolution. To deny its importance would be to commit the same error as those who wish it away with magic words of debatable meaning such as "corporatism," for example.

Capitalism has created an artificial world where mankind is maladjusted. The community is exploited by a narrow caste that monopolizes all power and aspires to international supremacy. Finally, capitalism hides under a debauch of new words, an anachronistic conception of the world where the economy explains everything. These criticisms also apply word for word to communism.

The solution to the maladjustment of mankind in a world that is not made for it is, as we have seen, a political problem. Technical and economic development does not justify itself, it is justified by its practical application. The new State will subject the economy to its own designs, to make it a tool of a new European spring. Creating civilized values, forging the weapons of power, and elevating the quality of the people, will then be its goals.

It is in a total transformation of the structure of the business (referring to business within the context of financial capitalism, not the small family business which must be preserved and where there is no problem) and the general organization of the economy that we will find the means to destroy the exorbitant power of the technocratic caste, to suppress the exploitation of the workers, to establish real justice, to rediscover true economy and healthy functioning.

In a capitalist regime as in a communist regime, the company is the exclusive property of the financiers in the former and the State in the latter. For the wage earners, be they managers or simple workers, the results are the same: they are robbed, the wealth produced by their work is absorbed by capital.

This privileged position gives the company power over capital: direction, management, even when they are barely involved and seek nothing but profit, sometimes even to the detriment of production and the enterprise itself.

The famous words of Proudhon find their full meaning here: "Property Is Theft!" To abolish appropriation is the solution that will lead to the community enterprise. Capital will then take its just place as an element of production, side by side with labor. The one and the other will participate, with a power proportionate to their importance in the enterprise, in the appointment of management, in economic management, and in the distribution of real profits.

This revolution in enterprise will fit in a new organization of the economy, having at its base the professions and the regional geographic framework. By doing away with the parasitic power of financiers, it will create a group of intermediary bodies. These new structures, capable of being easily integrated into Europe, can find no better definition than that of "organic economy."

A Young Europe

The American and Soviet victory in 1945 put an end to the conflicts between European Nations. Enemy threats and a shared fate in good and bad as well as similar interests have led to a general feeling of unity.

This feeling is confirmed through reason. Unity is indispensable to the future of European Nations. They have lost the supremacy of numbers; united, they would recover the strength of civilization, of creative genius, of organizing power, and of economic power. Divided, their territories are doomed to be invaded and their armies are doomed to defeat; united, they could form an unstoppable force.

Isolated, they will become mere satellites, doomed to fall, as some already have under Soviet domination. European civilization will come under systematic attack and it will be the end of mankind's evolution. United, they would have the means of imposing and of ensuring their civilizing mission.

Unity does not mean the continuation of financial and political organisms instituted after the war. Their purpose is to extend the international power of the technocracy and to preserve the political and economic privileges that are hidden behind the banners of democracy. These institutions create, on a European scale, the vices and words generated by each nation's ruling regime, and multiply them. The development of these institutions accelerates Europe's decline.

Unity does not mean leveling the field. Standardization and cosmopolitanism will destroy Europe. Its unity will be built around the national realities that each people intend to defend: historical community, original culture, attachment to the soil. To want to limit Europe to either Latin or Germanic influence would be to maintain divisions, and develop new hostilities. But above all, it would deny the European reality created by Rome and the medieval era in which its two currents, Continental and Mediterranean, met.

To imagine Europe under the hegemony of one Nation would re-open a bloody wound whose historical scars are still fresh.

The diversity of languages and origins is not an obstacle. Many States are multilingual, and the Roman Empire, which represents the first instance European unity with regard to the unification of peoples and their cultures, had Emperors born in Rome as well as in Gaul, Elyria, and Spain.

Europe's borders do not simply stop at the artificial boundary of the Iron Curtain imposed by the victors of 1945. It includes the totality of European nations and peoples. Thinking of unity is, first and foremost, to think of liberation for all the captive nations from the Ukraine to Germany. The destiny of Europe is in the East: breaking the chains, overthrowing the Soviet tyranny, and driving back the Asiatic tide.

Beyond the European continent, the people and states that belong to its civilization make up what is called the Occident. Europe is its soul. Its solidarity will assert itself, notably within the Occidental centers of Africa. These places are the bases for a new organization of the African continent, whose fate is tied to that of Europe.

In the construction of Europe, the underdeveloped peoples will find both an example to follow, and solutions to their own difficulties. It is not hand-outs that they need, but organization. Europe possesses an incomparable corps of groups that specialize in overseas matters. No other power could compete with the organizational talent of these groups, bolstered with the dynamism of an awakened Europe. They will take these people out of misery and anarchy and bring them back to the West.

Economic treaties will not unite Europe. The Nationalism of its people will. The obstacles that appear insurmountable only appear as such within democratic structures. Once the regime is swept out, these illusory problems will disappear by themselves. It is therefore obvious that without revolution, no European unity is possible.

The success of revolution in one European Nation — and France is the only one to possess all the necessary conditions — will allow for a rapid extension of it into other Nations. Two Nations independent of the regime will create such a seductive force of dynamism that the old system, the Iron Curtain, and the borders will collapse. The first step towards unity will be a political one, leading to the creation of a single collective state in an evolutionary form. The military and economic steps will follow. The Nationalist movements of Europe will be agents of this unity and will form the core of the future living European order.

Thus a Young Europe, founded on the same civilization, the same space, and the same destiny, will serve as the active center of the West and of the world order. The youth of Europe will have new cathedrals to construct and a new empire to build.

ORGANIZATION AND ACTION

The struggle for Algeria has shown that the "nationalists" can at least help create a favorable situation. But they have also shown (without going back to events prior to the Second World War) their total inability to transform a popular revolt into a revolution. An embryonic nationalist organization, despite their efforts, was unable to keep pace with the spontaneous revolt. Thus, "nationalist" conceptions prevailed, and new resistance engaged under more favorable political conditions after April 22, 1961, having both partisans and means, sank into ridicule and dishonor.

However, this period of clandestine struggle and repression forged many young, revolutionary combatants, and the circumstances in which that revolt collapsed provide a good lesson for those who placed their confidence in "nationalist" methods. This is why the Nationalist militants of the future will surpass those of the past.

The fight for the integrity of our nation's territory in Algeria will leave a profound mark on the French youth of today. The best among them were active participants. They risked everything, torture, prison, death. The condemnation of terrorist methods does not apply to those who fulfilled their orders and served as examples, but to the leaders who decided to use these harmful methods. The revolt of the Youth against a senile and hostile society is a reality.

Nobody foresaw the Poujadist tidal wave of 1955 or the peasant revolts of 1961. Despite their modern comforts, men, by the hundreds of thousands, went into the streets. The malfeasance of the regime will do nothing but create further popular revolts. These, like those before them, will fail due to their disorganization. Our goal for the future, then, is to introduce yeast into the dough.

Organization, penetration, and popular education, are always slow. We must not forget that all the revolutionaries of the twentieth century had to fight long and hard before they triumphed: Lenin fought close to thirty years, Hitler thirteen, Mao Zedong thirty-three... In the difficulties of the struggle, the masses acquire a revolutionary consciousness, new cadres emerge, the organization is broken in and is reinforced.

The development of revolutionary action is never progressive and harmonious. Like a broken line, it is made up of partial successes, setbacks, recoveries, of greater setbacks, periods of apparent stagnation. Every revolutionary movement has known catastrophic setbacks when victory seemed to be within reach: the Bolsheviks in 1905, the National Socialists in 1923, the Chinese Communists in 1927 and again in 1931. Their success was due to their ability to analyze the causes of these setbacks, to draw lessons from them, to correct their missteps, and to adapt to new conditions. The Bolsheviks abandoned their illegalist[2] policies in order to explore both legal and illegal opportunities. The National Socialists rejected the insurrectional path in order to undertake a legal conquest of power. Mao Zedong left the urban proletariat behind and chose to undertake towards guerrilla campaigns. Revolutionary action, like war, obeys certain laws. Nationalists must search for them in the light of their own experience and adapt them to new situations.

Notables or Militants

For a Man or an Idea?

The voter, the simple partisan, follows the headlines, listens to popular pundits, whoever the savior of the day is. The "nationalists" take full advantage of this. Passive herds, expect their miracle men to fix everything. Even the smallest groups have their idols. The inevitable disappearance of the great men leaves the naïve embittered and discouraged. The Nationalist does not need followers but militants who are defined by their doctrine, not in their relation to a man. He does not fight for a pseudo-savior, for the savior is found within himself. Those who a take the helm can disappear or make mistakes and they are replaced;

---

2   Illegalism is an anarchist philosophy that developed primarily in France, Italy, Belgium, and Switzerland during the early 1900s as an outgrowth of individualist anarchism. It openly embraced criminality as a lifestyle.

the value of the cause is not tainted by this. The militants sacrifice themselves for their ideas, not for a man.

An organization must be a community of militants, not someone's personal property. It should be managed by officials who serve as temporary spokesmen for Nationalism. These officials will direct the action of militants, because they will have been proven themselves to be the best qualified to serve the Organization, without which they would be nobody.

Bluffing and Effectiveness

The enormous sums of money collected in the fight for French Algeria were absorbed by the notables and the politicians to whom they were entrusted. All they produced in an attempt to justify their positions were a few pamphlets, conferences, travel, and some posters. With these colossal means at their disposal, the notables did nothing.

During this time, militants were developing a coherent plan of action with meager means coming only from their own personal contributions. They held public meetings, canvassed the country for members, made posters by hand, realized spectacular achievements with little money, used Roneos in every single corner of France. They achieved a lot with nothing. This I indicative of true militancy.

The Notables and the Rank and File

For the notables who direct the "nationalists," their militants are an inferior class. They are only the rank and file to be used for political struggles. They are simply electoral material. They are pawns in their plots. Their self-sacrifice serves as a stepping-stone for the ambitions of careerists. If the affairs turn out badly, the militants are quickly abandoned.

Nationalist Organizations will need to push aside the notables. Their members and leaders will be militants coming, not from the electoral laboratories or back alley plots, but from combat: nights of postering, public speeches, brawls, stormy meetings, printing leaflets on a Roneo[3] at night and distributing them at dawn, arrests, interrogations, brutalities, prisons, trials, disappointments, insults, indifference, setbacks... This is where you will find the most tenacious, the most devoted, the most conscious, here is where you will find the revolutionary elite.

Union of "Nationals" or Organization of Revolutionaries

Hidden Enemies

A number of politicians, civilian and military alike, have turned to Algeria as a springboard for their ambitions. Men of the regime, as a result of their training and interests, have remained sworn enemies of the revolution. They have been most suited to fighting it rather than supporting it. The Gaullists, certain

---

3   An old brand of copying machines using stencils.

members of parliament, and certain leaders thereafter, are perfect examples of the regime's infiltration of the revolt.

One of the plotters of May 13, Léon Delbecque, shamelessly made it clear: "I was the organizer of May 13," he declared on July 6, 1958, at the conference of the Social Republicans.

"In the offices I occupied, I was solicited to participate in plots often directed against the Republic and the republican regime, plots the police knew of but were unable to stop. I managed to be at the right place at the right time, allowing me to alert General de Gaulle to the existence of the uprising."

The directorate of the OAS was full of such individuals who "managed to be at the right place at the right time" to bring the revolt to a dead end. If the Secret Army had dethroned de Gaulle, the same individuals would have helped the regime weather this crisis without much fuss, as they did on May 13.

They are very good at using the confusion born of apparently similar goals. They know that the "nationalists," lacking as they are in political education, succumb to union blackmail and have a guilty fondness for their supposedly repentant adversary.

To accept their game would be to fall into their hands. Keeping quiet about their machinations is the same as complicity. No alliances with men of the regime! They must be denounced with the utmost vigor. With this, the masses will cease to be misled, partisans will lose their natural naïveté and will become educated militants.

Zero plus Zero

Zero plus zero always equals zero. Grouping mythomaniacs, plotters, nostalgics, careerists, and "nationalists" together will never yield a coherent force. Preserving the hope of uniting the incapable is to persevere in vain. The few elements of value are paralyzed by the cranks that surround them. Popular opinion is not mistaken here. Also, they do considerable harm to Nationalism, which they frequently misunderstand. They scare away the healthy elements and prevent the recruitment of quality militants.

Working with these types is out of the question. On the contrary, we must make the fundamental differences that separate them from Nationalism clear. The cranks must be pitilessly pushed aside. This way, it will be possible to attract new and effective partisans.

Unions and Committees of Agreement

Even the OAS, with its dynamic action, with its unique direction, its enormous means, and an essential common objective, did not succeed in rallying support for French Algeria in Metropolitan France. How can one think that a dream, as old as national opposition, can come to be in a future bereft of such favorable conditions?

Nationalist groups and fronts have but one goal, to benefit those who organize or control them. The Popular Front favored the communists, while the nationalists served Soustelle. The other participants were dupes.

Put forward by notables, groups and committees more often than not have an electoral goal. They get bill posters and crowd control teams at a premium; they make great cash siphons. When the electoral period ends, the group is put to sleep to await a new occasion to exploit the credulity of the "nationalists."

For example, the instant there is any real difficulty, a decision to be taken on a controversial event, the front explodes and everybody scatters. The dream ends. The political struggle, just like war, demands clever maneuvering: concealment, retreat, attack. It requires total discipline and a single leading force capable of taking initiative instantaneously, and engaging all its forces. The heterogeneous composition of these groups and the diversity of ideology among their leaders prohibit them from applying these laws; they are thus doomed to opportunism and disintegration.

How could an incoherent herd, dominated by blabbermouths, careerists, and weirdos, undermine the infighting, be capable of struggle against the superior organized force of the regime? The latter is not a goal for "nationalist" notables. This form of action is condemned by experience. Group tactics cannot be envisaged without a powerful Nationalist organization capable of imparting its élan and imposing its political line.

Monolithic and Disciplined Organization

The work achieved in the last few years was accomplished by small teams and isolated militants. This hard core was composed of educated, reliable, and competent militants. Their means were small, but their tenacity and imagination made them authors of all the partial successes recorded in the struggle.

There is proof that five militants are more valuable than fifty weirdos. Quality of combatants is, by far, preferable to their quantity. It is around a small and effective team that the masses will assemble, not the other way around.

That revolutionary movements are made up of effective minorities does not mean that all small groups are revolutionary. It makes an easy excuse for the mediocrity of certain groups. The most effective of these minorities are not sterile sects, they are in direct contact with the people.

Destined to fight, the Nationalist Organization must be one monolithic and hierarchical entity. It will be created when all the militants for the Nationalist cause have united. Their age, no more than their milieu, is of no importance. Be they students or peasants, workers or technicians, these militants will be propagandists and the organizers of the revolution.

Depending on the circumstances, their actions may or may not be overt. Their virtues will enable them to enter into the general population up to and including the mechanisms of the regime.

Plots or Popular Action

Behind the Times

Examples set by the Gaullist plots, the systematic terrorism of the FLN or of the IRA in Ireland, have appealed to a number of "nationalists." It is easier to copy the past than to imagine the future. Anachronism in politics, as in warfare, ensures defeat; one cannot conduct trench warfare in the age of tanks.

Certain images have caused great damage in the past. The Spanish Civil War, the national insurrection of 1936 around the army. May 13 and the military pseudo-revolt. The appeal to the soldiers, so dear to the "nationalists." The French army is a component of the regime; its chiefs have been carefully chosen for their self-interested submission, its cadres are, in majority, simply doing their jobs, but they are not the army with a capital A. The elements within the army that will help patch up the regime.

It is through lack of self-confidence and the rejection of effort that the "nationalists" have unloaded their responsibilities onto the blind hope of non-existent military plots. It is intellectual cowardice, a false excuse to escape from the patient and difficult task of militancy.

A Thousand Revolutionary Cadres

Popular consent is no more sufficient than action in the streets to assure the success of revolution in a technically developed society. There is no power without control, from inside the technical mechanisms that ensure the functioning of a modern State. The extreme complexity of the High Administration, its covert power, and its colonization by the caste of technocrats make it a world apart, impenetrable, and all-powerful. Only revolutionary cadres within these mechanisms, even in very small numbers, will neutralize and make it yield to nationalist will. Certain public services of vital interest for the functioning of the country, infiltrated by the technocrats and the communists, fall within the same framework.

In the open, as the standard-bearer of Nationalism, the political movement itself will have the task of publicly speaking to the people and winning them over. It will utilize all legal means of propaganda and action. Built on a hierarchical corps of educated militants, organized into territorial and professional cells, it will appeal for widespread support.

In overt or covert liaison with this political movement, "bases" will be progressively organized. As explained above, the purpose of these "bases" is to handle and control a specific milieu by way of social and political action, weeding out adversaries and absorbing neutral partisans. This work will give birth to diverse associations adapted to their particular milieus. It will rest entirely on the Nationalist cadres, who would be specialized and capable of looking after the organization.

Penetrating the mechanisms of the State and creation of a political movement and popular bases will be the principal goals of the Nationalist Organization. The latter will be built on a corps of hierarchical and specialized cadres, present in all social organizations, connected to a centralized leadership. The organization will thus be capable of orchestrating the same campaign throughout the country in all its aspects. It will be able to maneuver with discipline and promptness in battle. Cadres and militants among the people will be like the yeast in the dough. A thousand elite revolutionary cadres will bring victory to Nationalism.

On the Occidental Scale

An Exterior Lung

After the events of April 22, 1961, the fight for French Algeria received permanent and active support from various groups of Nationalists in Europe and even the United States. For the first time, Westerners stood in solidarity in spite of the borders that separate them.

These groups used their propaganda to support the militancy in France. Newspapers, brochures, conferences, meetings, demonstrations, support committees, all adopted the same watchwords.

Several Nations became, in a way, the exterior lungs of the French resistance, allowing it to regain its breath. Working groups were set up. Fugitive partisans were given lodgings. The regime understood the danger. It intervened on the diplomatic level to stop support for the French combatants and to repress acts of solidarity.

Solidarity and Orchestration

Faced with the permanent plotting of liberal regimes and the international communist organizations, the Nationalists of the West must not only persevere in this way, but also increase acts of solidarity. The militants of the European Nation must find seek out propaganda beyond their borders, propaganda that explains their struggle, exalts their courage, denounces the repression and the brutality of which they are victims, and awakens the sentiment of a common struggle among European peoples for their survival against those who want to enslave them.

The expansion of these initiatives must allow a true orchestration around a very simple central theme: struggle against communism and against all those who support it.

Through highly diverse channels — the press, student groups, unions, members of parliament, political movements, cultural associations, ex-servicemen, youth organizations, committees of intellectuals — a vigorous counterattack could be conducted against the Soviet enterprises and those who indirectly support them. An event demonstrating the collusion of the liberal regime and communism, or another capable of arousing popular indignation, could be orchestrated everywhere at the same moment. A coordinating body, giving each cell their freedom of action will have to collect information and distribute it for purposes of exploitation.

New Blood

Bringing the youth into the political struggle, the influence of struggles conducted in France, and various new issues have accelerated the need for a new definition of Nationalist ideology as a doctrine of a Young Europe. Numerous contacts, the exchange of ideas, and joint conferences have displayed an ideological convergence among European militants.

The last few years, which have been an incomparable source of education for the Nationalists of France, represent an unparalleled experience offered to the Nationalists of Europe. Here a method has been adapted to new conditions of struggle. In the positive critique undertaken by French militants, European combatants will find lessons that will guide their action.

To Begin

To begin we must create the conditions for a new, popular, and resolutely legal action. From this perspective, the last after-effects of the OAS, which from now on serve as a powerful asset of the regime, must be eliminated because they are harmful.

It is important to develop a positive critique of previous actions, to work collectively for a new definition of Nationalism. It is necessary to speak, to write, to explain, to request the use of the national opposition press for this work. All opportunities must be grasped and personal works must be inspired by this concern and in service of this need.

Propaganda must be pursued so as to maintain the presence of Nationalism. Crying over the past or practicing a policy of resentment would be counter-productive. The responsibility for the abandonment of Algeria lies, not with a misled people, but with the regime and the politicians (civilian and military) who directed the "nationalist" fight.

In the same way, it is necessary to maintain contact with all sincere partisans. To aid those who have suffered. To be actively present beside our refugee compatriots from Algeria and not leave the initiative solely to the forces of the regime.

This transitional period must be put to good so as to prepare for the time when once dispersed militants, get together so as to set up a Nationalist Organization, define its program, and begin the fight.

Plots do not solve anything, they are harmful. The conspirators resemble old maids who meet to vent their anger and resentment. Salon plotters or terrorists cut themselves off from their compatriots. They assume an attitude that will be misunderstood, they become bad-tempered, and resentment dominates them. They thus move away from Nationalism and victory.

Theatrical Revolutionaries

It is not the means, but the goals that characterize a revolutionary organization. The means, by themselves, are dependent on the circumstances. Thus, the Bolshevik party used illegality and violence, whereas the National Socialist party, also a revolutionary organization, used solely legal means to conquer power.

Extravagance in expression and the promise of Apocalypse, have never helped the Nationalist cause on the contrary. The enemy finds easy arguments, people avoid men who appear like dangerous fools, partisans then become discouraged or become deformed in their turn.

The theatrical revolutionaries, in their remarks, their attitude, and their action, are enemies of the revolution. In particular, the younger elements should be on their guard. Dressing in a costume, confusing sectarianism with intransigence, and displaying gratuitous violence are infantile practices. Some would find the exaltation of a morbid romanticism here. The revolution is neither a fancy dress ball nor an outlet for mythomaniacs. Revolutionary action is not the occasion for an increase in purism.

Bases Among People

Action aims to enlighten the people intoxicated by the powerful propaganda of the regime, to propound the nationalist ideal, and to organize for victory. This is why priority is given to propaganda. Directed at the masses, this action must be strictly legal.

Working among the people is not only for communists, all it takes is the right approach. Systematic and patient penetration will cover the most varied aspects. The discontent of workers in a company against the official unions, neighborhood housing protests the concentration of refugees from North Africa in a high density block of flats, an opening in a local federation of farmers, a student guild, the elections in a favorable municipality, an army instruction center, a professional school, there are so many opportunities to create nationalist "bases" among the people. The teacher, the engineer, the officer, the unionist, Nationalist militants, everyone is a potential organizer of these "bases." The organization of such bases in popular milieus implies a specialization of work and the concentration of efforts on a few points chosen after a thorough analysis of the chances and the means to be employed. Better to control just one company, one municipality, one university faculty, than to deploy a generalized agitation without any hold over the masses. These strongholds of Nationalism will become the best propaganda assets. They will be schools of militants and organizers who, in their turn, will pursue their work in other milieus.

It is a long and exacting struggle without glory and without panache. It is painstaking, but it is the only way.

Craft Industry or Effectiveness

Craft Industry

In the beginning, the Nationalist struggle, for lack of means, entrusted a very small group of militants with everything. What was necessary during the first stage becomes catastrophic when the organization develops. A few organizers are overburdened with innumerable activities, each of which is as necessary as the rest. Everyone begins to rely on them for everything. For fear of seeing a task poorly executed by a new member, the organizer continues to do everything by himself. The spirit of initiative disappears, and with it, the taste for action. The militants of value see themselves relegated to basic duties; they lose their faith and their dynamism.

In this craft industry stage, everybody must know how to do everything and nobody is responsible for anything in particular. The personal abilities of militants are ignored. Craft industry work leads to an extraordinary loss of energy and quality. Thus, one saw an excellent economic journalist, well connected in the United States, charged with distributing OAS fliers in post offices. He was arrested while undertaking this menial task that could have been given to a younger partisan, perhaps a high school student. His specialization was unique and was irreplaceable.

The overworked organizer and the unused militant share the same feelings of ineffectiveness and disgust. Both feeling as though they are working in a vacuum.

The tried and tested militants exist in sufficient numbers for the future Nationalist Organization to refuse suffocating craft industry work.

Division of Labor and Centralization

The variety of activities within an Organization, the diverse milieus that it must penetrate, the overt and covert character of the struggle, imposes a division of labor that must, in certain cases, be compartmentalized. This division into branches, entrusted to proven officials, is logically accompanied by a single and centralized command at the top.

Within each branch, the division of labor and the specialization of members must be the same. The local organizations must be able to devote themselves to the action, centralization, and specialization. For example, the propaganda branch should be able to rapidly supply material adapted to local groups, rather than over-generalized and locally irrelevant material.

Through its militants, the Organization must be present everywhere, including inside the adversary. The presence of militants in certain economic and administrative mechanisms can be of infinitely superior utility than their participation in the activities of an activist group. The struggle does not take a single form. This is why the division of labor must be equally applied at the level of local organizations. Members must be the active elements of a common struggle, responsible for specific tasks, and not simply executing orders. This is how effective militants, organizations, and cells will be formed.

OTHER BOOKS PUBLISHED BY ARKTOS

SRI DHARMA PRAVARTAKA ACHARYA	*The Dharma Manifesto*
ALAIN DE BENOIST	*Beyond Human Rights*
	Carl Schmitt Today
	The Indo-Europeans
	Manifesto for a European Renaissance
	On the Brink of the Abyss
	The Problem of Democracy
	View from the Right (vol. 1–3)
ARTHUR MOELLER VAN DEN BRUCK	*Germany's Third Empire*
MATT BATTAGLIOLI	*The Consequences of Equality*
KERRY BOLTON	*Revolution from Above*
ISAC BOMAN	*Money Power*
RICARDO DUCHESNE	*Faustian Man in a Multicultural Age*
ALEXANDER DUGIN	*Eurasian Mission: An Introduction to Neo-Eurasianism*
	The Fourth Political Theory
	Last War of the World-Island
	Platonic Politics
	Putin vs Putin
	The Rise of the Fourth Political Theory
KOENRAAD ELST	*Return of the Swastika*
JULIUS EVOLA	*Fascism Viewed from the Right*
	A Handbook for Right-Wing Youth
	Metaphysics of War
	Notes on the Third Reich
	The Path of Cinnabar
	A Traditionalist Confronts Fascism
GUILLAUME FAYE	*Archeofuturism*
	Archeofuturism 2.0
	The Colonisation of Europe
	Convergence of Catastrophes
	Sex and Deviance
	Understanding Islam
	Why We Fight
DANIEL S. FORREST	*Suprahumanism*

OTHER BOOKS PUBLISHED BY ARKTOS

ANDREW FRASER	*Dissident Dispatches*
	The WASP Question
GÉNÉRATION IDENTITAIRE	*We are Generation Identity*
PAUL GOTTFRIED	*War and Democracy*
PORUS HOMI HAVEWALA	*The Saga of the Aryan Race*
RACHEL HAYWIRE	*The New Reaction*
LARS HOLGER HOLM	*Hiding in Broad Daylight*
	Homo Maximus
	Incidents of Travel in Latin America
	The Owls of Afrasiab
ALEXANDER JACOB	*De Naturae Natura*
JASON REZA JORJANI	*Prometheus and Atlas*
	World State of Emergency
RODERICK KAINE	*Smart and SeXy*
LANCE KENNEDY	*Supranational Union and New Medievalism*
PETER KING	*Here and Now*
	Keeping Things Close: Essays on the Conservative Disposition
LUDWIG KLAGES	*The Biocentric Worldview*
	Cosmogonic Reflections: Selected Aphorisms from Ludwig Klages
PIERRE KREBS	*Fighting for the Essence*
STEPHEN PAX LEONARD	*Travels in Cultural Nihilism*
PENTTI LINKOLA	*Can Life Prevail?*
H. P. LOVECRAFT	*The Conservative*
CHARLES MAURRAS	*The Future of the Intelligentsia & For a French Awakening*
MICHAEL O'MEARA	*Guillaume Faye and the Battle of Europe*
	New Culture, New Right
BRIAN ANSE PATRICK	*The NRA and the Media*
	Rise of the Anti-Media
	The Ten Commandments of Propaganda
	Zombology

OTHER BOOKS PUBLISHED BY ARKTOS

TITO PERDUE — *Morning Crafts*
William's House (vol. 1–4)

RAIDO — *A Handbook of Traditional Living*

STEVEN J. ROSEN — *The Agni and the Ecstasy*
The Jedi in the Lotus

RICHARD RUDGLEY — *Barbarians*
Essential Substances
Wildest Dreams

ERNST VON SALOMON — *It Cannot Be Stormed*
The Outlaws

SRI SRI RAVI SHANKAR — *Celebrating Silence*
Know Your Child
Management Mantras
Patanjali Yoga Sutras
Secrets of Relationships

TROY SOUTHGATE — *Tradition & Revolution*

OSWALD SPENGLER — *Man and Technics*

TOMISLAV SUNIC — *Against Democracy and Equality*

ABIR TAHA — *Defining Terrorism: The End of Double Standards*
The Epic of Arya (2nd ed.)
Nietzsche's Coming God, or the Redemption of the Divine
Verses of Light

BAL GANGADHAR TILAK — *The Arctic Home in the Vedas*

DOMINIQUE VENNER — *The Shock of History*

MARKUS WILLINGER — *A Europe of Nations*
Generation Identity

DAVID J. WINGFIELD (ED.) — *The Initiate: Journal of Traditional Studies*

Made in the USA
Middletown, DE
28 October 2023

41487746R00038